Merlin

QUICK STARTER   250 HEADWORDS

Great Clarendon Street, Oxford, OX2 6DP, United Kingdom

Oxford University Press is a department of the University of Oxford.
It furthers the University's objective of excellence in research, scholarship,
and education by publishing worldwide. Oxford is a registered trade
mark of Oxford University Press in the UK and in certain other countries

First published in 2014

2018 2017 2016 2015 2014

10 9 8 7 6 5 4 3 2 1

ISBN: 978 0 19 424974 4   Book
ISBN: 978 0 19 424957 7   Book and MultiROM Pack

MultiROM not available separately

Printed in China

This book is printed on paper from certified and well-managed sources

ACKNOWLEDGEMENTS

Illustrations by: Oliver Cuthbertson/The Bright Agency

DOMINOES

Series Editors: Bill Bowler and Sue Parminter

Merlin

Janet Hardy-Gould

Illustrated by Ollie Cuthbertson

Janet Hardy-Gould has worked as a teacher of English for many years. In her free time she enjoys reading history books and modern novels, visiting other European countries, and drinking tea with her friends. She lives in the ancient town of Lewes in the south of England with her husband and their two children. She has written a number of books, including *Henry VIII and his Six Wives* and *King Arthur* in the Oxford Bookworms series, and *Ali Baba and the Forty Thieves*, *Crying Wolf and Other Tales*, *The Great Fire of London*, *Sinbad*, *Mulan*, *Hercules*, and an adaptation of *Sherlock Holmes: The Emerald Crown* in the Dominoes series.

OXFORD
UNIVERSITY PRESS

Story Characters

Merlin

Merlin's father

Adhan

Vortigern

Ronwen

Ceridwen

Morfran

Arwel

Contents

BEFORE READING

1 Match the words in the box with the characters. Use a dictionary to help you.

> a bully   an enchantress   a king   the king's wife
>
> a magician   a princess

a Adhan is.................................... . **b** Merlin is.................................... .

c Vortigern is................................ . **d** Ceridwen is................................ .

e Morfran is.................................... . **f** Ronwen is.................................... .

2 Which person in this story does this? Write the names.

    a He learns magic from books, and helps the king. ....

    b He laughs at Merlin, and says bad things to him. ....

    c He fights his enemies in the east of his country. ....

    d She changes into different animals, and runs angrily after Merlin. ....

    e She teaches her son about different plants in the forest. ....

    f She asks for a beautiful new castle. ....

Chapter 1
The boy Merlin

castle a big old building; a rich person lives here

princess an important woman in a small country

king the most important man in a country

kingdom the country of a king

fight to hit someone again and again; when you hit someone many times

forest a place with lots of trees

plant a small green thing, with leaves, and sometimes with flowers

hunter this person looks for and kills animals

enchantress a woman who does unusual things that you can't explain

Ceridwen /keˈrɪdwen/

Young Merlin lives in a **castle** with his mother, **Princess** Adhan. The castle is in Wales, in the west of **King** Vortigern's **kingdom**. Merlin doesn't know his father. He's **fighting** for the king far away.

The castle is near a **forest**. Merlin and his mother often walk there. She teaches him about forest **plants**.

'When you're older, you can come here without me,' she says. 'But be careful. There are many **hunters**. And an **enchantress**, Ceridwen, lives here, too.'

Merlin's only friend is a **toad**. One day, Merlin visits the village near the castle. Two boys, Morfran and Arwel, are behind him. But Merlin doesn't see them. He talks to his toad.

'Merlin's talking to his toad!' Morfran laughs.

'Go away,' Merlin says. 'Or when my father comes back home . . .'

'We're not afraid, Merlin. Your father's never at home,' Arwel says. 'And is he truly your father? Perhaps you're a **demon's** child!'

That night, Merlin tells his mother everything. 'What can I do about these boys?' he asks.

READING CHECK

Choose the correct words to complete these sentences.

a Merlin lives with his *father* / *mother* in a castle.

b Merlin's father is always *far away* / *at home*.

c Princess Adhan and Merlin often walk in the *forest* / *village* near their home.

d *The enchantress Ceridwen* / *Princess Adhan* lives in the forest.

e Merlin *has* / *hasn't* got a lot of friends.

f Merlin has got a *toad* / *dog*.

g One day, two boys *fight* / *laugh at* Merlin.

h The boys say bad things about Merlin's *father* / *mother*.

i Merlin *speaks* / *writes* to his mother about the boys.

GUESS WHAT

What happens in the next chapter? Read the sentences and write 'yes' or 'no'.

a Princess Adhan talks to Morfran and Arwel. ………

b Merlin's father speaks to him one night. ………

c Morfran and Arwel find Merlin again. They kill his toad. ………

d Merlin walks away from the boys, and goes far into the forest. ………

Chapter 2
The bullies come back

'I can talk to those **bullies**,' Princess Adhan says.

'No,' Merlin answers. 'They call me a "mother's boy" without that!'

'Then your father can speak to them after he comes home,' she smiles. 'But be careful with Morfran. He's Ceridwen's son.'

Next week, Merlin goes to the village shop with his mother. He sits near the door with his toad in his hand. Suddenly, Morfran and Arwel **jump** out in front of him. 'It's Merlin and his toad!' they cry.

bully (*plural* **bullies**) a person who does bad things to somebody and makes them feel afraid; to do bad things to somebody and make them feel afraid

jump to move suddenly from one place to a different place

fall to go down suddenly

ground we walk on this

The toad is afraid. It **falls** to the **ground**. 'Let's see your toad jump!' Morfran laughs. He runs after it.

When Merlin's mother arrives, the bullies leave.

That night, Merlin sees his father in a **dream**. He is sitting under an **oak** tree after a fight with the king's **enemies**.

'I'm dying,' Merlin's father tells him.

'Father, no! I need your help with some bullies!' Merlin cries.

'When they bully you, walk away,' his father says. 'Look for the biggest oak in the forest. There's something important near it.'

dream pictures that you see in your head when you are sleeping

oak a kind of big tree; we often find them in England

enemy (*plural* **enemies**) someone who is not a friend

cauldron a large pot that an enchantress uses for cooking things over a fire

Next morning, Merlin tells his mother about the dream. 'Listen to your father,' she says quietly.

When Merlin meets the bullies again, they take his toad. 'Say goodbye to Mr Toad!' Morfran laughs.

Merlin remembers his dream, and walks into the forest. He lives there for days, and eats forest plants.

Then, one day, he finds the biggest oak in the forest. There's a little house near it. In front of the house, there's a boy. He's sitting near a **cauldron**.

'Who's that?' Merlin thinks.

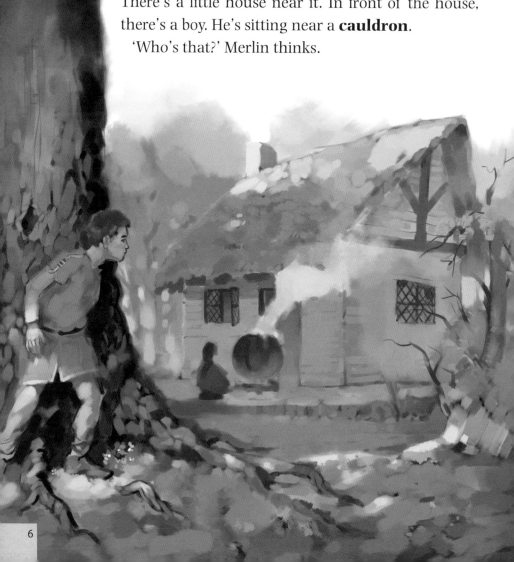

READING CHECK

Match the first and second parts of the sentences.

a Princess Adhan wants to speak to ———

b Merlin and his mother go to

c The bullies jump out in front of

d In a dream, Merlin sees

e Merlin's father is dying after a fight with

f The bullies take

g Merlin goes into the forest, and lives on

h In the forest, Merlin looks for

i When he finds the tree, he soon sees

j In front of the house, there's

1 Merlin's toad.

2 the bullies.

3 a boy.

4 plants.

5 the village shop.

6 the biggest oak.

7 a little house.

8 Merlin.

9 his father.

10 the king's enemies.

GUESS WHAT

What happens in the next chapter? Tick the boxes.

a From behind a tree, Merlin sees…
  1 ☐ Morfran.
  2 ☐ Arwel.
  3 ☐ a young demon.

b In the cauldron, Merlin finds…
  1 ☐ some cold water.
  2 ☐ some hot milk.
  3 ☐ a warm drink.

c After Merlin drinks, he…
  1 ☐ dies.
  2 ☐ changes a lot.
  3 ☐ sleeps on the ground.

Chapter 3
Ceridwen's magic potion

Merlin watches the house from behind the oak tree.

'Morfran!' a woman cries through the open window.

'Yes, Mother,' the boy says. The woman comes out of the house.

'Oh no!' Merlin thinks. 'It's Morfran, and his mother – the enchantress Ceridwen.'

'Is the potion ready?' Ceridwen asks.

'Soon, Mother,' Morfran answers.

'This **potion** can give **magic powers** to the first drinker of it!' she cries. 'And that is *you*, my son!'

Morfran smiles.

'I need to find a bottle. Then you can drink the potion from it. We must do it quickly, before your father comes home,' Ceridwen says. She goes back into the house.

Merlin moves nearer, but Morfran doesn't see him. Just then, Morfran takes something out of a little bag.

'Oh, no!' Merlin thinks. 'It's my toad!'

'Ha! Ha!' Morfran laughs. 'Here's one more thing for the potion!'

'Stop!' Merlin cries. He jumps out and takes the toad from Morfran. But at the same time, he hits the cauldron with his leg. It goes over onto the ground. Some of the potion falls onto Merlin's hand.

potion
something that you drink to give you magic power

magic
something that makes things happen in a way that you don't understand; making things happen in a way you can't understand

power being able to make somebody or something do what you want

'Merlin!' Morfran cries angrily.

Merlin smiles. He moves his hand up to his mouth.

'Wait!' Morfran cries. 'Don't drink that!'

light this stops a place being dark

But Merlin quickly puts the potion in his mouth.

Suddenly, a magic white **light** comes from Merlin's head. Just then, Ceridwen comes out of the house with a bottle in her hand. She sees and understands everything. She looks angrily at Merlin.

'You must die for that!' she cries.

READING CHECK

Are these sentences true or false? Tick the boxes.

	True	False
a Merlin sees Morfran and his father at the house.	☐	☑
b There is a something magic in the cauldron.	☐	☐
c Ceridwen is making a potion for Merlin.	☐	☐
d Ceridwen goes back in the house, and looks for a book.	☐	☐
e Morfran wants to put Merlin's toad in the potion.	☐	☐
f Merlin's leg hits the cauldron.	☐	☐
g Some of the magic potion goes onto Merlin's leg.	☐	☐
h When Merlin drinks the potion, a light comes from his head.	☐	☐
i Morfran now has magic powers.	☐	☐
j Ceridwen is very angry with Merlin.	☐	☐

GUESS WHAT

What magic power has Merlin got in the next chapter? Tick one box.

a ☐ He can understand his toad when it speaks.

b ☐ He can change into different things.

c ☐ He can make money.

d ☐ He can call demons to him.

Chapter 4
Merlin runs away

'Come here, boy!' the enchantress cries.

'I need to run!' Merlin thinks. In his head, he sees a **hare**. Then, suddenly, he is a hare.

'Aha!' he thinks. 'So now I can change into different **animals**.'

Merlin runs away into the forest. 'I can easily run faster than Ceridwen now,' he thinks.

But when he looks behind him, he sees a big dog. It is running after him, and its angry mouth is open.

'Oh, no!' he thinks. 'Ceridwen can change into different animals, too.'

hare an animal like a big rabbit; it has long ears and it can run very fast

animal a living being that moves; a dog or a cat is an animal

Merlin moves quickly through the trees. But he can hear Ceridwen behind him. She is coming nearer.

Just then, he arrives at a **lake**. 'I need to be a **fish**,' he thinks. Suddenly, he's a long, dark fish. He moves fast through the cold water of the lake.

'I'm all right now,' he thinks. But when he looks back, an **otter** is coming through the water behind him.

'Ceridwen's an otter now!' he thinks.

So he changes into a little **bird**, and goes far up into the sky. But soon he hears an angry cry behind him. Now a big **eagle** is coming after him.

lake a lot of water with land around it

fish an animal that lives in water

otter a small, brown animal; it lives in rivers, move very fast, and eats fish

bird an animal that can fly through the sky

eagle a very large, strong bird

arrow you shoot things with this

'Ceridwen again!' Merlin thinks.

He moves here and there in the sky, but he can't lose the eagle. Just then, Merlin sees a hunter far down in the forest, and there's a sudden noise – '*Whoosh*!' An **arrow** hits Ceridwen. She falls to the ground near her house. Morfran runs to her dead body.

'Merlin, you demon!' he cries angrily. 'One day you must die for this!'

READING CHECK

Correct the mistakes in these sentences.

a Merlin can now change into different ~~people~~. *animals*

b Merlin first changes into a cat, and runs into the forest.

c Morfran can change into different animals, too.

d Merlin soon arrives at a sea, and he goes into the water.

e In the water, Merlin is a fish, and Ceridwen is an eagle.

f Next, Merlin goes far up into the hills.

g Then Merlin sees a princess down in the forest.

h An arrow suddenly hits Merlin.

i Morfran is very angry because his mother is ill.

GUESS WHAT

What happens in the next chapter?

Morfran finds one of his mother's old potions, and…

a ☐ he kills Merlin with it.

b ☐ he changes into a true magician.

c ☐ he gives it to the king's new wife when she is ill.

Chapter 5
King Vortigern's castle

After some years, Princess Adhan – Merlin's mother – moves away to a **convent**. But Merlin stays in his father's castle. He reads books, and works on his magic powers. 'I want to be the best **magician** in the kingdom,' he says.

At first, Merlin learns to change the **weather**. Next, he learns to see through **walls**. Then he learns to look into the **future**.

convent a church building where women live and work away from the world

magician somebody that makes things happen in a way that you don't understand

weather when there is sun or rain, and it's hot or cold

wall the side of a building; something that keeps bad things away

future the time after now

Morfran lives with his father in the forest. He often thinks about Merlin.

'Perhaps I can kill him with one of my mother's old potions,' Morfran tells his friend Arwel.

But the old potion bottles have nothing in them – all but one. 'And this potion doesn't kill people,' Morfran says. 'It makes ill people well again.'

'So give it to somebody important,' Arwel answers, 'and **pretend** to be a magician.'

pretend to do things to make people think that something is true when it isn't

Soon after that, King Vortigern visits Wales after years of fighting. He has a new **wife**, Ronwen, but she is ill. Morfran hears about this. He goes to the king's men with the magic potion. Ronwen is well again after she drinks it. So Vortigern calls for Morfran.

'You can be my magician!' the king says.

Ronwen is happy in Wales. She wants to stay there. 'Let's make a castle on this hill!' she tells Vortigern.

Vortigern begins the new castle, but the walls fall down again and again. 'Make a magic potion and stop this!' the king tells Morfran.

'I need the **blood** of a boy without a father for that,' Morfran answers. 'Now, the son of a demon lives near here. Give me some men, and I can bring him to you.'

wife a woman living with a man

blood this is red; you can see it when you cut your hand

READING CHECK

Choose the right words to finish the sentences.

a Merlin works on his magic powers, and he learns to change… .
   1 ☐ the time   **2** ☑ the weather   **3** ☐ people's dreams

b Ceridwen's old potion can make people… .
   1 ☐ happy   **2** ☐ ill   **3** ☐ well

c Morfran gives the potion to… .
   1 ☐ King Vortigern   **2** ☐ the king's wife   **3** ☐ Merlin

d Morfran is now the king's… .
   1 ☐ friend   **2** ☐ hunter   **3** ☐ magician

e Ronwen speaks to the king. She wants a new castle… .
   1 ☐ on a hill   **2** ☐ in a forest   **3** ☐ next to the sea

f When Vortigern builds the castle, all the … suddenly fall down.
   1 ☐ king's men   **2** ☐ walls   **3** ☐ trees in the forest

g For his potion, Morfran wants the … of a boy without a father.
   1 ☐ blood   **2** ☐ hair   **3** ☐ eyes

GUESS WHAT

In the next chapter, there are two dragons. What do they do? Tick two boxes.

The two dragons…

a ☐ fight angrily under the hill.

b ☐ change into Vortigern's enemies, and fight him.

c ☐ suddenly run at the king's wife, and kill her.

d ☐ breathe fire on Morfran, and kill him.

e ☐ eat Merlin and King Vortigern alive.

Chapter 6
A true magician

Vortigern's men bring Merlin to the hill.

'Here's the demon's son!' Morfran tells Vortigern. 'Kill him. I can make a potion with his blood, and put it on the ground. Then you can finish your castle.'

'Morfran's my enemy! And he's wrong!' Merlin cries. 'There are two **dragons** under the hill. I can see them through the ground.'

dragon a big animal that can fly through the sky and send fire from its mouth

'Dragons?' Vortigern asks.

'Yes,' Merlin cries. 'A red dragon and a white dragon. When they fight, the walls fall down.'

The dragons hear Merlin's cries, and they come up angrily through the ground. They are fighting, and **breathing fire** and smoke

'I can stop them!' Morfran says. He pretends to do some magic, but he is not a true magician. The dragons breathe fire on Morfran, and kill him.

Merlin quickly changes the weather. Suddenly there's a wall of rain in front of the dragons. They move up into the sky. When the rain goes, the dragons are far away.

'You're a true magician!' Vortigern cries.

He finishes his castle, and calls for Merlin. 'Tell me about the future!' the king says.

breathe to push air or fire from your mouth

fire this is red and hot and it burns

Merlin closes his eyes. 'You, Vortigern, die without any children,' he answers. 'Dark years of fighting come after that. Then I see a sword with magic light in it, a king with a wonderful castle, and his beautiful wife. I'm that king's magician.'

'Be my magician!' Vortigern cries.

'No,' Merlin answers. 'I must work more on my magic. I must be ready when my king and my country need me.'

Then Merlin changes into a hare, and runs away into the forest.

READING CHECK

Put the sentences in order. Number them 1–9.

a ☐ Merlin makes a wall of rain, and the dragons go away.

b ☐ The king's men take Merlin to the hill.

c ☐ Vortigern now understands – Merlin is a true magician.

d ☐ Merlin tells the king about the dragons under the ground.

e ☐ Vortigern wants Merlin to be his new magician.

f ☐ The dragons suddenly come up through the ground.

g ☐ Merlin tells Vortigern about the future.

h ☐ Merlin quickly changes into a hare, and he runs away.

i ☐ Morfran speaks to the dragons, but they kill him.

GUESS WHAT

What happens to Merlin after the story ends? Tick 'yes' or 'no'.

Merlin …   Yes   No

a learns a lot more magic, and helps people. ☐ ☐

b changes into a bad man, and kills people. ☐ ☐

c lives quietly in the forest, and makes potions with plants. ☐ ☐

d helps a famous king. His name is King Arthur. ☐ ☐

e learns to fight, and fights all the king's enemies. ☐ ☐

f finds a wife, but she is a bad enchantress. ☐ ☐

g has many children with magic powers. ☐ ☐

h is soon the most famous magician in the country. ☐ ☐

23

Project A *A magician or enchantress*

1 Read about Merlin. Complete the table.

Merlin is a famous magician, and there are many wonderful stories about him. He comes from Wales, and he is the only child of Princess Adhan and Prince Meurig.

Merlin has got many magic powers. He can change into different animals, look into the future, see through walls, and change the weather.

When Merlin is older, he is a good friend to King Arthur, and to all the men of the Round Table. He helps Arthur to fight his enemies, and to be a good king.

His enemy is the enchantress Morgana le Fay. At first, he loves her, and he teaches her magic. But soon she uses bad magic on him, and he is very angry with her.

At the end of Merlin's long story, he doesn't die. He goes to sleep in a magic cave. One day, he must wake from his sleep, and help his country again.

Name and job	Merlin – magician
From	
Family	
His different magic powers	
Friends	
Enemy	
What happens in the end	

2 Read the notes in the table, and complete the text about Morgana le Fay.

Name and job	Morgana le Fay – enchantress
From	Cornwall – in the west of Britain
Family	Parents – Duke Gorlois and Lady Igraine; sisters – Elaine and Morgause; half-brother – King Arthur.
Her different magic powers	She can make people well again when they are ill. She can make potions, become different animals, and fly.
Friends	Guingamar – King of the Island of Apples
Enemy	Merlin and Arthur
What happens in the end	She takes Arthur in a magic boat to the Island of Apples.

Morgana le Fay is an enchantress, and you can read many interesting old stories about her. She's from .... in the .... of ...., and she's the daughter of Duke .... of Cornwall and his wife, Lady .... Morgana has two .... – Elaine and Morgause, and she has a ...., too. His name is ...., and later, he's the .... of Britain. Morgana has the power to make .... people well again. She can make magic ...., change into different ...., and .... quickly through the sky. Morgana's friend is .... He is the King of the .... People sometimes call this magic island 'Avalon'. Morgana is the enemy of the magician .... For many years, she is angry with her half-brother, ..., and he is her enemy, too. But in the end, Morgana helps Arthur when he is dying. She takes him in a .... to the .... Arthur stays on the island. One day, he must come back, and be the king of his country again.

3 **Find out about more famous magicians or enchantresses on the Internet. Write notes about them.**

Medea

Nicholas Flamel

Dr Faustus

Baba Yaga

Circe

4 **Choose one magician or enchantress from activity 3. Write a short text about them. Use the texts in activities 1 and 2 to help you.**

Project B *A letter from a story character*

1 Merlin's father, Prince Meurig, is writing to his wife, Princess Adhan. Complete the letter with the words in the box.

| answers at home books |
| boys castle fighting forest |
| friends questions village |

Dear Adhan,

I can't stop thinking about you and Merlin **a)** . . . . I want to come

back when we stop **b)** . . . . , and see the two of you again.

I often think about our beautiful **c)** . . . . , and the wonderful things

near it. Do you go for long walks in the **d)** . . . . with Merlin every day?

Does Merlin talk to you more now? Does he have any new **e)** . . . . ?

Perhaps there are some nice **f)** . . . . in the **g)** . . . . , and he's

friends with them.

Can Merlin read and write now? Which **h)** . . . . does he like best? And is

he a good student?

Write back soon. I'd like to know the **i)** . . . . to all my **j)** . . . .

I can't wait to hear from you.

With love,

Meurig xxx

2 Read Adhan's answer to Meurig's letter. Find seven more mistakes in her letter.

Dear Meurig,
                    letter
Thank you for your ~~picture~~. Of course, I think about you all the time, too.

Yes, Merlin and I drive in the forest every day, and I teach him about the dragons there.

He's very interested in them.

Merlin talks to me a lot now. He has many friends in the village. His only true friend is a

bird. There are some girls in the village, but they aren't very nice. They help Merlin when

they see him, and he is very afraid of them, I think.

Merlin is phoning a lot now. He likes old French story books. And he can write well, too.

How are things with you? When are you coming home?

Please answer soon!

Love,

Adhan xxx

3 **When Princess Adhan goes to the convent, she writes to Merlin. Order the questions in the box to complete her letter.**

> are / doing? / How / you
>
> happy? / you / Are / feeling
>
> go for a walk / Do you / every morning? / in the forest
>
> well / eat / every day? / Do you
>
> from the village shop / buy food / every week? / Do you
>
> nicer to you / that boy Morfran / Is / these days ?
>
> have / new friends? / any / Do you
>
> now? / learning / Are you / more magic
>
> can / different things / What / you do ?

Dear Merlin,

Things are nice here at the convent, but I think about you every day, and I have a lot of questions to ask you!

First of all, ...

..

I often think about our visits to the forest.

..

What about food? ....

..

..

And that bully? ....

..

..

What about your work? ....

..

That's all for now! Write to me soon, and answer all my questions.

Lots of love,

Mother xxx

4 **Swap your letter with a different student in the class. Read the letter you get. Imagine you are Merlin. Write his answer.**

WORD WORK 1

1 These words don't match the pictures. Correct them.

a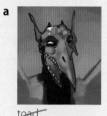

~~toad~~
..... demon .....

b

princess
....

c

castle
....

d

forest
....

e

plant
....

f

jump
....

g

oak tree
....

h

cauldron
....

i

king
....

j

fight
....

k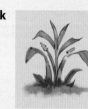

demon
....

l

hunter
....

2 Complete the sentences with different words from Chapters 1 and 2.

a She's an ... enchantress ... . She can change into different things.

b When I have a bad ...., I often call for help in my sleep.

c 'Has your country got a king?' 'Yes, it has. It's a .... '

d 'Look at me, Mum! I'm up this tall tree!' 'Be careful! Don't ....!'

e 'Where's my bag?' 'It's on the .... at your feet.'

f 'Is that boy nice?' 'No. He's a ...., and he sometimes hits me.'

WORD WORK 2

1 Find words from Chapters 3 and 4 in the cauldrons to match the pictures.

a kael ....lake....

b sfhi ....

c troet ....

d algee ....

e wraro ....

f reah ....

2 Complete the sentences with different new words from Chapters 3 and 4.

a It's dark in this room. We need a l i g h t.

b Merlin has a new _ _ w _ r. Now he can change into different things.

c We've got two dogs, three cats, and a horse at home. We've got a lot of _ n _ m _ _ s

d Can you hear the _ _ r _ in that tree? It's singing beautifully.

e There's a p _ t _ _ n in this bottle. When you drink it, you change into a toad!

f That enchantress loves reading books about _ a _ i _ .

29

WORD WORK 3

1 Complete the words from Chapters 5 and 6 to match the pictures.

a m. agician.....

b f.................

c w.................

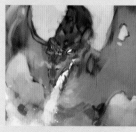

d d.................

e w.................

f b.................

2 Complete each sentence with these new words from Chapters 5 and 6.

breathe   convent   future   pretends   wife

a Merlin's mother goes and lives quietly in a .. convent.... .
b My teacher's over there with his .... She's wearing a red coat.
c 'What do you want to do in the ....?' 'I want to be a singer.'
d My grandfather never walks fast because he can't .... very well.
e When my little brother doesn't want to do something, he .... to be ill.

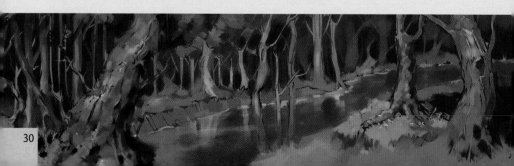

GRAMMAR CHECK

Present Continuous: Information and *Yes/No* questions

For Present Continuous questions, we use the auxiliary verb be and the –ing form of the verb.

Information questions begin with a question word – what, where or who. The subject comes after the verb be and before the –ing form of the verb.

What is Ceridwen doing?   *What are the dragons breathing?*   *Where is Morfran running?*

For *Yes/No* questions, we re-use the verb be in the answer.

Is Morfran sitting near the cauldron? Yes, he is.

1 Look at the picture. Write the Information and *Yes/No* questions

a where / the toad / sit?

......Where is the toad sitting?......

b where / the king's men / stand?

....

c the king / sit / on a chair?

....

d the dragons / breathe / fire?

....

e who / the king / watch?

....

f Morfran / run away?

....

g who / call / the dog?

....

h the king's men / fight?

....

2 Match the questions in activity 1 with the answers.

1 [c] No, he isn't.   **5** [ ] No, they aren't.

2 [ ] Morfran.   **6** [ ] Under the oak tree.

3 [ ] On Merlin's head.   **7** [ ] One of the king's men.

4 [ ] Yes, he is.   **8** [ ] Yes, they are.

GRAMMAR CHECK

Adverbs of frequency

We use adverbs of frequency to show how often something happens.

always   often   never

       usually   sometimes

These adverbs go after the verb *to be* but before other verbs.

Morfran always listens to his mother.

Merlin and Princess Adhan often walk in the forest.

The bullies are sometimes in front of the village shop.

Merlin's father is never at home.

3 **Choose the correct adverb of frequency from the words in brackets. Put it in the correct place in each sentence.**

        sometimes

a Princess Adhan ∧ visits the village when she goes out. (sometimes / always)

b Merlin talks to his toad. (often / never)

c Morfran and Arwel are nice to their enemies. (never / usually)

d Ceridwen changes into an eagle. (sometimes / always)

e The dragons kill their enemies with fire. (usually / never)

f Vortigern is the most important man in his kingdom. (often / always)

4 **Complete Merlin's diary with adverbs of frequency.**

I don't know my father because he's a) ..... *never* ..... (0%) at home.
He's b) .... (100%) away fighting for King Vortigern. But
Mother is here all the time. We c) .... (60%) visit the forest
next to the castle, and she d) .... (30%) teaches me about
the plants there. On Mondays, I e) .... (90%) walk to the
village with her, and I f) .... (100%) take my toad 'Tom'
with me. Tom is g) .... (90%) very good, but he
h) .... (30%) jumps off my hand when he's afraid.

GRAMMAR CHECK

The possessive 's

We use the possessive 's to show that something belongs to somebody.

Perhaps you're a demon's child!

Merlin stays in his father's castle.

With singular nouns, we add 's: *Ceridwen's cauldron, Merlin's toad.*

With most plural nouns, we just add ': *those dragons' eyes* (= more than one dragon), *the boys' teacher* (= **many boys**), *the babies' hats* (= more than one baby)

With irregular plural nouns, we add 's: *the women's faces, the children's coats*

5 Match the people or things on the left with the people or things on the right.

a	Merlin	**1**	wife, Ronwen
b	King Vortigern	**2**	mother, Adhan
c	the men	**3**	fire and smoke
d	Morfran	**4**	fat, green body
e	the dragons	**5**	friend, Arwel
f	the toad	**6**	horses

6 Write the phrases from activity 5 with 's or '.

a Merlin's mother, Adhan

b ....

c ....

d ....

e ....

f ....

7 Put ' in these sentences where necessary.

a Those boys' homes are in the village.

b Ceridwens son is the kings new magician.

c The bullies names are Morfran and Arwel.

d Morfrans mother has got magic powers.

e That hares legs are very long.

f The birds are afraid of those hunters cries.

33

DOMINOES Your Choice

Read *Dominoes* for pleasure, or to develop language skills. It's your choice.

Each *Domino* reader includes:
- a good story to enjoy
- integrated activities to develop reading skills and increase vocabulary
- task-based projects – perfect for CEFR portfolios
- contextualized grammar activities

Each *Domino* pack contains a reader, and a MultiROM with:
- an excitingly dramatized audio recording of the story
- interactive games and activities to improve language skills

If you liked this Quick Starter Level *Domino*, read these:

The Sorcerer's Apprentice
Retold by Bill Bowler

'What's your job?' Yukio asks.
'I'm a sorcerer,' the old man smiles. 'And I need a young apprentice.'
One day, Yukio – a young boy from old Japan – leaves his sister in the country and looks for a job in the town. He finds interesting work there, as a sorcerer's apprentice. But why must Yukio wait to learn magic? And what happens after he puts a spell on a broom when the sorcerer is away?

Crying Wolf and Other Tales
Aesop

'Help! A wolf is eating my sheep!'
What happens when a bored shepherd boy lies to the people in his village – and then he later tells the truth?
What do a man and his wife do when their goose lays golden eggs? And what can two travellers learn from a bear in the woods? These three Greek tales teach us important truths about people today.

	CEFR	Cambridge Exams	IELTS	TOEFL iBT	TOEIC
Level 3	B1	PET	4.0	57-86	550
Level 2	A2–B1	KET-PET	3.0-4.0	–	390
Level 1	A1–A2	YLE Flyers/KET	3.0	–	225
Starter & Quick Starter	A1	YLE Movers	1.0–2.0	–	–

You can find details and a full list of books and teachers' resources on our website: www.oup.com/elt/gradedreaders